For Freya-Rose, Elias and Ada

First published in Great Britain in 2022 by McKenzie Publishing House.

A catalogue of this book is available from the British Library.

ISBN: 978-1-7399253-2-1

Enjoy! Kaana

Annie lived on the top of the hill,
And had so much wool she could barely stand still!
She often wobbled from left to right,
Teetering and tottering from morning to night.

Until one day she had had enough,
She had to get rid of the excess fluff!
She packed the only scissors she could find,
Knitting needles too – they couldn't be left behind!

And off she went, hoping to see,
Someone - anyone - to help in her time of need.
Wobbling here and wobbling there,
Anybody would do - she really didn't care!

And presently then a figure came into sight,
Could this be the one – could they be just right?
Annie introduced herself with a sweet, 'Hello,
I think, Mr Pig, there's something you should know.'

‘As you can see, my wool is so thick,
I can share it with you – I can cut it off quick.
I’ve scissors in my bag – knitting needles too,
Whatever you need I will knit for you.’

'Knit for me? But I don't need any wool,
Just look at this weather – it's beautiful.
Go on your way now and find someone new
And knit for them whatever you want to!'

So Annie took off, feeling quite down,
She couldn't shake off her sad little frown.
Until the day another figure came into sight –
Could this be the one? Could they be just right?

Annie introduced herself with a sweet, 'Hello,
I think, Miss Pony, there's something you should know.
As you can see, my wool is so thick,
I can share it with you – I can cut it off quick.
I've scissors in my bag – knitting needles too,
Whatever you need I will knit for you.'

Miss Pony replied, 'I don't need any wool,
Why would I need it? I wouldn't look cool.
Now, off you go, please, I'm busy today.'
And dropping her head, she went on her way.

So off Annie went, feeling quite sad,
Her wool was growing longer – it really was bad.
She didn't want to waste it, to throw it away,
She wanted to be generous and make someone's day.

Why had Mr Pig and Miss Pony been so rude?
Annie always tried her best to be as kind as she could.
But she had to accept that not everyone's the same,
And it wasn't her fault – she wasn't to blame.

And true as the day turned into night,
Soon winter's chill came and gave everyone a fright.
Annie's wool grew much heavier than before,
And the snow kept falling more and more.

Back in the woods Mr Pig began to quiver,
Miss Pony was the same – she shivered and shivered.
They remembered the clothes Annie had offered to knit,
And agreed they had to find her,
'Come on, quick, quick!'

They searched high and they searched low,
Trudging through the deep and cold snow.
They were ever so sorry for being rude,
Something woollen and warm would be oh, so good!

Then one night they happened to see,
Annie Alpaca, as lonely and as big as can be.
She turned around and couldn't believe her eyes,
It was rude Pig and Pony – the two who had made her cry.

They offered their apologies and said how sorry they were, Annie was very forgiving - she was that kind of girl. And once they hugged and had a good chat, Annie got to work and made them the most wonderful hats.

And now Annie is so well known in town,
Knitting for the village and neighbouring surrounds.

She's extremely happy keeping everyone warm,
And that is the secret to her beautiful, kind charm.

SPOT THE DIFFERENCES

Spot 6 differences in the below pictures